AF264301

Copyright by author Mercedes Webb-Pullman

ISBN 978-0-9922629-8-3

Let's hear it for the girls

poems by

Mercedes Webb-Pullman

Table of contents

After Goldilocks

Momma Bear thinks Goldilocks should be
locked up. She's angry. Baby Bear misses
his friend. He liked having someone smaller
in the house.He's sad. Poppa agrees with Momma
for the sake of peace. He doesn't believe it's Goldi's fault.

What kind of parents wonders Momma *let
a child that age go walking in the woods,
alone?* She's disgusted. Baby Bear doesn't
like being alone much, doesn't understand
people afraid of the woods. He's confused.
Poppa hums. He's not investing in this situation.

Goldi's mother, frantic when Goldi didn't
come home, called the police. They found her
deep in the forest, in bed with a young bear.
Two adults were asleep in the same room.
Arrested, charged with unlawful imprisonment,
the Bears engaged the Hells Angel's lawyer.
He was sharp, and cheap.

She broke and entered, why wasn't she charged?
Momma won 't let it go. *Who's going to pay for
the broken chair? When will Baby get his bed-clothes
back from forensics?* The rape charge was dropped
after Goldi underwent physical examination by
a Court-appointed doctor. *I don't mind sleeping
on the rug beside my bed.* Baby Bear tries peace.

Poppa Bear, who's usually just right, wants them
to think about it from a sociological point of view.
*Remember, we're three hairy homosexual males
who ride motorbikes. They don't understand us,
they've never seen gay men make a family before.
Just be glad we got off lightly. Home detention -
no problem in winter, we'll hibernate at home.
And maybe it's time to look around for a little
baby sister bear for you, son. Momma is a great
little mother, for a man.*

Amelia

Pidge, don't cry!
The box broke, but I
am fine. I can fly!

My head throbs. Blood
in my mouth. I mustn't smile,
they tell me, or the gap shows.
Not elegant.

Drainage-tube-in-my-cheekbone
ache. The little red plane, choosing
me at the Toronto Expo,
didn't mention this.

Pidge, salt and sand
taste the same, everywhere.
So does blood.

I flew all around the world
to find Long island again.It's certainly
not long now. Am I still
on the other side of the imaginary lion?
Is that why everything is so
topsy-turvy?

Solo. Doing it alone. Lindy did.
They called me Lady Lindy once.
I still miss my little yellow canary.

Fred's sulking, he won't answer me.
No one will answer me. Some sort of
navigator hc turned out to be. As a flyer
he'd make an excellent sailor.

Solo. Fred's gone swimming. I saw him
floating away. I'll cook some fresh fish,
have a nice dinner ready when he returns.
Waiting. I have unlimited hours now.

The white of the seagulls dazzles me,
their brutal blind eyes.

Anaïs

me
me me me me
me Guiler me Miller
me my father me me me
Allendy me me Rank me me
me my patients me me me me
me Steinbeck me Artaud me Wilson
me me Vidal me Agee me Herlihy me Durrell
me me me Bridget me me June me me
me Moré me me Rainer me
me me me Pole me me
me me me me me
me me me
me

Anne Sexton, listening to the devil

The devil stays silent,
harsh as a mountain cliff-face.
Rigby, uglier than a husband,
fiddles with machines in the workshop,
mumbling. I exhale a peppermint breath
benediction. He works in stained overalls,
curses the devil through his dry lips,
cracked by chemical vapours and sun.
He barks 'Why?' like an angry parent
already discounting any reply.
He's formal and hostile.
The devil lies right under our feet.

Everyone thinks they'd recognise
his appearance, even without a body.
He didn't have a body when I was a teen.
Then, he was tiny, hiding in dark cracks
in the floorboards, ready to leap, a spider's hunger.
As a child, I thought unborn babies
hid there with him, among lost hairpins.
Then, my pillow was as soft as a breast,
and inside, winter fires purred. Rigby,
when he gets here, ask him ...
Dammit Rigby,
ask him why life breaks me down.

Annie

Oakley shot a squirrel
in the house, through the orchard,
to get a hickory nut.

A rifle fired writing
side to side.

The encyclopedia failed,
her audience truly split
edge-on, tossed in the air, cigarettes
from lips, a card riddled
before it touched the ground.

Perhaps her ability to repeatedly
touch, while using feet.

R. A. Koestler-Grack watched
Chief Sitting Bull. Oakley
skipped her rifle,
aimed at a candle,
snuffed out the whizzing bullet.

Chief Sitting Bull watched corks off bottles,
a cigar held in his teeth.

Antigone

Death upon death upon death
stretch out behind me. I come
from a blood-thirsty family,
punished by Gods through
generations.

My father Oedipus was also my brother.
He'd killed his father the King, claimed
his mother the Queen in marriage. He
didn't know.

When my mother learned she'd married
her own son, her husband's murderer
had fathered her children, Jocasta
killed herself.

She'd tried to circumvent the prophesy
by disposing of her first-born son. He lived.
came back. Can the Gods ever be tricked,
or appeased?

Blinded by anguish, Oedipus left his kingdom
to his two son/brothers, to share year-about.
My brothers killed each other in battle.

My uncle Creon claimed Thebes, called
my brother, Polydices, a turncoat, refused
to allow his body burial rites. When I tried
he arrested and imprisoned me.

Did I actually bury him? Or, did I throw
his ashes to the wind? Did this happen while
Oedipus still reigned? I hanged myself.

I was to marry my uncle's son Haemon.
He saw my body, joined me in death.
When she learned, his mother, my aunt
Eurydice, killed herself.

Or, did Dionysus intervene, and Haemon
and I were married?

Or, did Haemon rescue me from his father,
hide me in a shepherd's hut to give birth
to our son Maeon?

Was Maeon recognized by a dragon's mark?

Did Heracles plead with Creon to spare our lives,
in vain?

Did Haemon then kill us all, so no one
got out of this
alive?

Do the Gods ever wonder why?

some Bessie blues (for Jan)

Beale Street blue Mama blue
standin' in the rain blue
aggravatin' Papa blue
me and my gin blue

eavesdropper blue
thinking blue
there'll be a hot time blue
Alexander's rag time blue

see if I'll care blue
outside of that blue
ain't nobody's business blue
dirty no-gooder blue

keep it to yourself blue
my sweetie went away blue
oh Daddy blue
I've got what it takes blue

do your duty blue
you've got to give me some blue
I'm wild about that thing blue
baby won't you please come blue

put it right here blue
baby doll blue
mean old bedbug blue
squeeze me blue

St. Louis gal blue
Chicago bound blue
worn out Papa blue
yellow dog blue

young woman blue
bleeding hearted blue
whoa Tillie take your time blue
cake walking babies blue

blue spirit blue
at the Christmas ball blue
nobody knows you when you're blue
rocking chair blue reckless blue

back water blue bo'weavil blue
muddy water blue safety blue
Gulf Coast blue hard time blue
careless love blue

don't cry baby blue
gimme a pigfoot blue
send me to the 'lectric chair blue
yodeling blue

my man blue poor man blue
preachin' the blues blue
lost your head blue
Sam Jones blue

empty bed blue
Mama's got the blues blue
graveyard dream blue
Devil's gonna get you blue

a good man is hard to find blue
I ain't got nobody blue
down hearted blue
cemetery blue

Jane Bowles

If I still wrote it would be of you
Cherifa. You in the black niqab
and sunglasses, you in my bed,
wanton as Tangier's cracked black
nights. My tropical illness.

Fever. The room fills with bugs, bats,
empty bottles; parasitical elevators
lead to the desert. The wind wild-imp-nervous.
The derangement of salvation.

You place spells, blood, in my houseplants.
Small skeletons and knots. You bring drums
from the medina. I shall suffer.

Detachment, starvation under sheltering
sky. My head stopped ticking. Self-indulgent
decadence, more kif, more gin. The Indian
trying not to look at me.

For years, Paul, for years and years I forged
my own hammer and nails.
You eclipsed me.

Cleopatra's suicide soliloquy

A cooler evening breeze brings
tatters of music, battle cries;
my final night in Alexandria.

Pan abandoned Anthony;
he died, just now, as I held him.
His gods all are fickle. I am Isis.

My life lies behind me, a tapestry;
queen and goddess, mother and wife,
twice lover of Imperial Rome.

Smoke shrouds the lighthouse,
light glows along the quay, like
the night Caesar fired our ships,

bright against a reddened sky.
Loud with battle, the crowd.
I strain to hear

last echoes of one exquisite tune
that curls and floats, fragile as ash
through the air.

your lover was here, now he's leaving

This is my punishment;
to be aware of time's paradox
so at this moment

all possible moments exist
except Mark Anthony,
turning back. I face

only endless night, as the sound
of my lover, leaving forever,
slowly fades away.

Coco

Although I couldn't sing a note in tune
it wasn't for my voice they filled the room.
Life's easier when wealthy friends can help
with details. Power loosens knots as well.
An orphan, convent raised, I stayed alive
with thread and scissors, lucky number five.

A wealthy lover passed me to his friend,
debauched aristocratic Englishman
who set me up in Paris. Luxury
soon put to flight the nun's frugality.

As miliner, society knew me,
then suits and dresses, perfume, jewelery,
as I moved on to conquer Russian Dukes,
composers, dancers, artists, Ballet Russe,
the Prince of Wales, young Churchill, Picasso,
and Goldwyn (though I hated Jews). Garbo
and Dietrich best of Hollywood's sparse fare,
its vulgar unrefined *vin ordinaire.*

I introduced Visconti to Renoir,
drank Brut champagne at noon in my pegnoir,
indulged in reverie with Revardy,
designed a double meaning with Iribe
and took a spy as lover, military
intelligence that keep me in the Ritz
for war's duration. Purgers had to quit
when Cooper intervened. If not, maybe
I'd have my head shaved. That could ruin me,
the empire I'd amassed. Someone stepped in
but to protect investments, or for friend
I never knew. White petals wilted on
black dresses, death and romance, siren song.

For almost eighty years my Number Five
has kept the scent of women vibrant, live
inside exquisite costly glass, remote
from time, and age; a melting winter note.

Effie

Louisa, you look so well! The new hat
suits you. Oh, and you owe me five guineas.
Remember you wagered that Victoria
would never receive Lady Millais
as long as Ruskin, her first husband, was alive?
Yet there she was, today.

I know an annulment is not the same
as divorce, but Victoria is prudish. I tried
to explain the difference; she wouldn't listen.
Effie curtsied happily enough, when she
was still married to Ruskin.

I can't help wondering what they did for six years,
sharing the same bed. Her grounds were 'incurable
impotency'. Two of London's best doctors attested
she was still a 'virgin entire'.

Something's strange about their situation.
Ruskin introduced her to protegé Millais.
Threw her at him, some say.
Ruskin never remarried, though he courted
more very young girls after Effie left. Some say
he can love only virgins; that's why he couldn't
consmuate.

He wrote her that odd book, when she
was only twelve years old. All those Pre-
Raphaelites were funny about young girls.
Even Millais. Some say there was something
odd about his relationship with Effie's sister,
Sophy. The beautiful one who died mad.

Then Effie and Everett had eight children.
Nothing wrong with her body. Victoria made Millais
a hereditary Baron eventually, so Effie became
Lady Millais. Victoria still refused to meet her
until Millais, on his death bed, was asked,
by Princess Louise, if Victoria could do anything
for him. 'Yes' he replied. 'Receive my wife'.

She did, took her curtsy forty years after
they'd last met. And I won our wager.
I think I'll buy a new hat, too.

Frida grieves

Trotsky attacked in Fortress Home.
He died this morning. If you hadn't
given him sanctuary with us in Mexico
maybe Piochitas would have lived.
Estupido, Diego. Who betrayed him?

Your affair with my sister Cristina
betrayed me. I walked out, cut my hair,
but couldn't function without you.
You catted around, so I did too.
Leon loved me without constraint.

We'd leave the Blue House separately,
meet in secret at the house you gave Cristina.
We played, excited, like naughty children
hiding from the world. I even hoped
you'd seduce Natalie.

Politically you and Trotsky moved apart;
soon he and Natalie left the Blue House.
Now he's dead. Of all the weapons
available to this assassin, he chose
to insert the pick of an ice axe
through Trotsky's head.

Just one small nip.

Georgia O'Keeffe 1918

From first solo exhibition in New York
to Spanish influenza, near death,
in weeks. A vortex. Behind me
I felt my body drain away
like water down a sink. Ahead
a curving corridor, a light,
brighter and warmer as I neared.

Music. A choir?
Is that my brother welcoming me?
Tugged back, grey, aching,
I sank, the light faded.

New York is built of light and shade,
ephemeral, two dimensional, without
empty space. No quiet. No peace.

Today I began an affair with Stieglitz.
Now bells ring out, sirens blare.
Not for us. The war has ended
over there.

Yes, very alien, Gertrude

Nine dry me
in my ermine finery;
my talent rent a little,
nail gone flinty but a Key
Largo wheel dents deep.
Sheep rings. Loss -
o well. We wire hats
to caps. Otto doesn't.
Toby leases peas,
Theo leaps lcas.
The ales please
and you pee
and they pee
the ease.

The girl who won't speak

She doesn't look at where their house once stood,
refuses to acknowledge home was there.
The crater has been filled, the grounds sits bare.
Her brothers will rebuild; cement and wood
they barter for already. This is good,
their thoughts are on the future. She can't bear
to think about what happens next, or care
to help her brothers, even though she could.

Their mother died there, just three months ago.
The children were at school when missiles hit
and coming home, found rubble still aglow
and all their world had changed. She tied a fray
of fabric from the shroud into a bow,
won't speak, just fondles it, and looks away.

Grendel

My grandmother's dragon lived
in her kitchen stove, with a black
lighthouse on the oven door.
Grendel breathed flames
and burned if you came too close.

When Grandma baked
she fed pine twigs so the fire
spat and roared, while flour,
sprinkled on an oven tray,
darkened from white
through cream to brown,

hot enough for scones
just before black;
then Grendel starved
and fell silent, smoldering.

Sometimes when I wake
from a dream, as it drains away
I think I can hear

some half-forgotten
starving thing,
still patiently breathing.

Henrietta Lacks

The end's like knotting off a cotton thread;
a length is finished, still the spool remains.
I live on through my children, though I'm dead.
My daughters have my lips, I smile again.
Through each maternal ancestor a chain,
our line unbroken since the first live birth.
Our DNA, as memory, prevails.
I never thought to travel round this earth.

From Africa, where life began, we spread
as servants, slaves, our treatment inhumane
with hunger, floggings, hanging overhead.
White masters took their pleasure in our pain
and bred our daughters. Lords in their domain
they knew exactly what our lives were worth.
They farmed us, sold our children. Some were slain.
I never thought to travel round this earth.

Then slaves were freed, to own their own farmsteads
and generations worked without complaint
to buy a patch of land, put up a shed
and grow a crop to sell, somehow maintain
a full-time job as well. Our pride shines plain
in children reading, learning, sounds of mirth.
The Good Book teaches 'Give, and you shall gain.'
I never thought to travel round this earth.

My cancer didn't die with me. Mundane
as my life's been, I somehow earned rebirth,
my stolen cells immortal now, arcane.
I never thought to travel round this earth.

Hillary's collections

Stones, feathers, shells,
cardboard cut from cigarette packets
and covered in her writing.

Each day she spends time
bent over them; selects, rejects,
 moves, makes room.

I knew a musician in Cooma
who kept collections.

He wrote a small card
for each person he saw
on his morning walks,

laid them out in random patterns,
introduced them to each other,
chatted.

He pulled down kitchen walls,
pinned cards between his house's ribs
on the inside, using push-pins
with different coloured heads.

After deliberating
he would change the colours,
or the cards, or both, or neither.

I think he'd understand Hillary,
why today, the display near her door
is all telephone numbers.

Yesterday it was messages
from Jesus, which are now
on the floor near the new
autumn-yellow leaves
set out in careful rows
beneath the window.

The legend of Hinemoa

She stares over water, shivers
with it in the breeze.
The island where Tutanekai waits
has vanished in evening mist,
a pale rainbow imprisons the moon.
The canoes have all been hidden.

She craves the wild honey
of his lips again, hot pepper
spicing their tongues,
the salt-bitter tang of his skin.
Almost she can taste him,
pungent and sweet.

Wood-smoke from his island
wafts by. She can smell
the fern and manuka
aroma of his hair, his breath's
karapapa blossom fragrance
as he whispers *Come to me!*

Over the sound of ripples
lapping, she can hear
the high sweet note of his flute.
The trees around her sigh,
murmur in time to his tunes.
Her pulse deafens her.

Her toes uncurl; she steps
into water so cold it burns.
It climbs her legs, scalds her breast
as she swims, grips her neck.
Muscles cramped, lungs aching
she struggles on towards her love,
or death.

Katherine Mansfield

Wellington London Brussels
Wellington Urewera London
Paris Scotland Brussels
Bavaria Bad Wörishofen
London Rottingdean
Cheyne Walk Greys Inn Road
Ditchling Bruges
Geneva Paris Oxford
Runcton Chancery Lane
Paris Cholesbury
Baron's Court Broadstairs
Ireland Paris
Rue de Tournon London
Chelsea Cornwall
Rose Tree Cottage Gray
Paris St Johns Wood
Cassis Bandol Marseille
Redcliffe Road Looe
Portland Villas Italy
San Remo Casetta Deerholm
Menton L'Hermitage Villa Flora
Villa Isola Bella
Switzerland Chalet des Sapins
Paris Switzerland London
Pond Street Paris
Le Prieuré

Russian New Year with Gurdjieff

She insists she feels better
but after she runs
up the long staircase
to her bedroom on the first floor
quickly without
holding the banister
Katherine collapses.

Moonlight catches in
blood streaming from her mouth
like flickers of fire -
hand to her lips, she coughs -
bright arterial flame
gushes from her lungs
I believe...

how she burns! The heat,
the fever. She drags each breath
through bubbles; her whole chest
boils, constricted, she feels
nothing can expand,
her heart must crack
I believe...I am going...

Helplessly
her fine privacy invaded
with nightmare clarity
the viscose crimson
oozing through her fingers
there is no more
famous author
just a frightened child
eyes wide
...to die..

Leni

We'd started shooting my movie
in Spain, but war moved us back
to Germany. I'd cast gypsies
in important roles. The Third Reich
paid all my bills. Grocer Goebbels
offered me prisoners, no employing
paid extras. They were in the camps
already. I didn't put them there.

I chose them myself, from the temporary
prison at Maxglan, filmed them in the Alps,
dancing; visions of joy and purity connected
to the mystic, majestic mountains, not
the grubby struggle on the plains.

Difficult filming, placing a camera on rails
to follow movement. Cutting these with
slow motion shots, high and low angles,
panoramic aerial shots, tracking shots
for following fast action. Always
running behind schedule.

The script called for more gypsies, in the
interior scenes shot at Babelsberg. This time
I chose from inmates of the Marzahn prison.
When I'd finished with them, they went back
to their camps. I realize now that most
went on to Auschwitz.

I didn't at the time. I couldn't change
what happened.

*I was one of millions who thought Hitler had
all the answers. We saw only the good things,
we didn't know bad things
were to come.* *

Lilith

Primeval Mother breathed the world, and we
were formed from the beginning, unified,
one consciousness, both male and female, tied
by caretaker's responsibility
'til Adam, greedy, shunned equality.
He wanted less than partner. How he tried
to subjugate me, husband over wife
until I grew new wings so I could flee

for safety far from Eden. When I'd gone
he set above the world an angry man,
replaced our Mother's love with strident spite,
declared me evil, called me Satan's spawn.
I know he's guilty, fearful; understand
that's why he says I visit him at night.

Malala

Malala blogged the truth. Some hated that;
her words made fools of local Taliban,
while overseas, important diplomats
supported her and her outspoken stand.

A teenage girl fell victim to a plot
to close her school, so women couldn't learn.
A bullet in her head, a brutal shot.
Assassination, point of no return.

But Allah intervened; Malala woke,
recovered, found a way to reach out far,
addressed the world, raised funds each time she spoke,
for schools for girls. A saint with battle scar.

When heroines are forged from circumstance
how can we know the dancer from the dance?

The Margaret collection

My neighbours in Systrum Street

Because her daddy loved her
and it hurt, the State
took Margaret away.

Her next daddy loved her
the same, his sons as well,
until it didn't hurt.

She left at sixteen, drifted off
to Kings Cross, a beat on the street,
a habit; life was brutal, as she'd expected
'til she fell in love with Warren
who married her.

They worked together; she
turned tricks, he helped her
as the house bouncer.

They dreamed of Lebanon;
her blue eyes and blonde hair
a Big Rock Candy Mountain
of easy money there,
and the world's best smack.

'Couples with similar interests
who work together for a common goal
are more likely to have
a stable and enduring relationship'.

Margaret

Her hands have held so many men
they feel nothing anymore;
to her the world is made of cocks
unconnected to hearts or minds.
She shoots herself up in my kitchen.

Mechanically she works her beat,
turns and returns to the same spot
as if some program permits her
just this distance and no more;

as if invisible bars cage her.

Her gaze, focused on an inner world
slides over faces sightlessly
like the eyes of an ancient statue
empty beyond even death.
Her husband waits at home.

Warren

Sunday afternoons he'd bang on my door
Lend us twenty bucks, she won't get up
and he was off to score a whack,
just to get her moving.

She used to be pretty. Not any more.

It was hard to watch, even when
I didn't really know them.
She could have been my sister.

He robbed someone, bought tickets
to Lebanon, *We'll make big bucks there,*
they'll love you but cashed them in to score
before the plane was due to leave. Someone saw
his picture on a police station poster. Wanted.
For robbery though, not murder.

Margaret was just another
dead junkie.

Marie

I'm tired all the time. They tell me *Rest*.
Lately I haven't been able to work, and
there are still new worlds to learn. I'm only 67.

Mostly TB cases crowd Sancellemoz Sanitarium.
They remind me of my mother, dying in Poland
last century. She'd have been proud of me;

her daughter discovered the cure for cancer.
Pierre, you were fortunate; alive one second,
dead the next, none of this erosion of faculties.

I found myself patting my pocket today, absent-
mindedly checking for a phial of radium.
My fingers still sting. The scars from holes

that ate into my flesh often redden and itch.
I have a feeling there's something important
I've missed.

The execution of Mary Queen of Scots

Queen of four countries, thrice wed,
double-crossed by cousin Elizabeth,
you leave your throne to your son in stead,
walk straight and serene to your death.

Like a bride, so serious and pale,
focus of eyes, you descend the steps
head held high. Your coif's veil
shines nuptial white through the depths

past balustrades wreathed in black
that match your satin velvet gown.
Shadows stretch behind you, back
to your father's death, your first crown

at six days old, through all the deaths along
your life. A petticoat shows a hint of red
below your dress; red as your hair once shone,
red as the sign of a martyrs death,

red as the blood that gouts and flows
over the dias where still you kneel
after the executioner's stroke.
Your blood stains your missal and rosary,

drips from your neck as he picks up your braid,
the watchers' horrified screams wide-spread
as your wig gives way, and over the stage
bounces your grey, cropped head.

Mary Tudor's madrigal

When I was Queen of England, Naples, Spain,
the Kingdom of Jerusalem as well,
I sent eight hundred Protestants to Hell,

revived the church that lust destroyed. In vain
heretics tried to hide; their numbers swelled
when I was Queen of England, Naples, Spain,
the Kingdom of Jerusalem as well.

I changed the laws my brother made. Sustained
by Christ I closed their churches, citadels,
took their convents and their castles. Bells tolled knell
when I was Queen of England, Naples, Spain,
the Kingdom of Jerusalem as well.
I sent eight hundred Protestants to Hell.

Meenybradden lady

My story is lost in time's fog.
No gravestone have I, to grow moss,
in the unhallowed ground of this swamp.
Eternally silent, time is a drip
of vinegar, pickling through layers of peat
to my dark airless tomb. The chill

of this valley's not nearly as chill
as the church's hypocrisy. Fuming a fog
of censure, they buried me here in the peat,
away from the churchyard, its crosses, the moss
on stones and oak. The diamonds that drip
from the railings when frost has covered the swamp

at sunrise, run down the hill to my swamp
bringing traces of corpses to wash me, a chill
rejoining of family. I feel them drip
to settle around me, hidden in fog,
holding me prisoner under the moss,
in death as in life. While harvesting peat

a peasant uncovered me, rolled back the peat.
He thought I was sleeping, there in the swamp
on mattress of peat, with blankets of moss,
and he pitied the lady asleep in such chill.
He wrapped me in wool, to stay warm in the fog,
and laid me back down. I saw moisture drip

from his face, but the mist here makes everything drip
and he may not have cried for me, sleeping in peat,
for I'd taken my own life. Locked in a fog
of lies and perversion, a bestial swamp
that my husband controlled, I prayed in the chill
of confession for help. I may as well ask moss

as it clings to the steeple. No parson, that moss,
but more honest. His threats, like acid, still drip
through my soul. I burned. Death's final chill
released me from fires much hotter than peat
but my soul's stuck here in this freezing swamp.
For centuries now I've called out through the fog:

Moss makes my blanket, my mattress is peat,
my tears drip into the swamp
where I sleep, in the chill, in the fog.

Mileva

For years we faced each other
across our massive square table
under the kitchen light.
Seated, I didn't limp
as we climbed towards
the unknown. Our theory
disproved simultaneity.
We'd hiked through fogs of old ideas,
but when we came into the clear
you stood on a separate mountain.

I lost our daughter
and my physics career
to your year of wonders.
I got older, ugly you said.
What wife could stand aside
passive and quiet
while her husband made love
to another, younger woman?
You called it 'the dark Slavic part'
of my soul, and never forgave me
my outburst against Anneli.
Destroyed your peace of mind, you said.
What about mine?

Jealous of science, yet I became
pregnant again. In Prague
where you were celebrated and I
knew no one, people treated me coldly.
You called me schizophrenic. I didn't
satisfy you in any way. You found marriage
an unbearable fetter. You saw
your 'beloved street urchin',
our 'great bohemian adventure',
as attempts to make something lasting
out of an accident. *You called our love
an accident.* You left me
with the speed of light.

Patti snaps from the M Train

10

three white fans two white skylights
white muslin drapes
solitary radiance
anywhere

20

sun slipped contraband
stripped and shackled
white gloves surrender
black coffee blue butterfly

30

lines invoking slaughter
glowing bookcase carved in bone
cold red sequined minidress
minutes deflating silver

40

iron rods resting miles
from the western edge
aesthetic holy grail delivered
figurehead girl with golden hair

50

a sealskin coat cracks floats away
ice tilts on the back of a whale
Icelandic pony brown the last
not lost moment mercifully

60

hard opportunity crazier than my conscience
glass of honesty by the elevator
floral bedspreads a worthy dialogue
impossible elderberry water close-up

70

ZZZZZZZZZZZZZZZZZZZZZZZZZZZZZZZZZZZZZZZ

80

a little red house on the side of Norway
translucent tentacles fron a jellyfish's bell
red rosebuds in the series of plankton
float in memory disappear in time

90

high fever navy blue and orange
speed ahead long-legged and free
a code word solemn knobs
entering our three-way portal

100

portal too sacred to fill
no time to wait forever
guuided by the page paper battle
at the end a grave

110

pearls drop scales of sorrow
water congregating frenzied
sugar grass cracked leaves
heaven not earth revolutionary

120

slain child left to rot in junkyard
moon spotlight on laughter
breeze exploding unscathed
rinsed out hanging pulled into sleep

130

strip hull scour cabin wax and polish wood
broken resources rare thing covered
with a tarp a piano sonata
rain steadily falling

140

mountain cliff a prayer a weapon
toss it away without flinching
empty sad paperback mascot
stone and book what did it mean

150

power and destruction boardwalk gone
gone motion roads closed wind strong

I flew to Madrid bus to Valencia
a restaurant called Juanita a mirror

160

quenching thirst a poet gave me years ago
a gift without hesitation or regret
I lost everything to protect me
in this short span it disappeared

170

rusting barges a dream silence
time grew closer where I live aloud
flannel shirts slightly musty held
by a green silk headscarf hung to dry

180

itinerary first dinner much sake
special soba solitude severed
an aspirin graves temples in the snow
correspond with my desires

190

white-cloaked mountain catastrophic sadness
a thousand paper cranes rice fields unyielding
a million fish carcasses rotting bitter cold
how to take a picture of nothing

200

by the sea where salt winds spiral
a notebook ribbon a cotton sock
Gothic ruins by the grave
a rare peace Spanish pilgrims

210

ZZZZZZZZZZZZZZZZZZZZZZZZZZZZZZZZ

220

Paul Bowles Tangiers 1997

230

Fathers Day Lake Ann Michigan

240

shedding shroud linen strips of hell
a Flemish Madonna who slept with the devil
the lost are found the dead
lifted into the arms of light

250

Virginia Woolfe's walking stick

Patty Hearst

The most well-known female bank robber
after Bonnie Parker
as long as the enemy exist
I can find no rest

after Bonnie Parker
the biggest action since Foster
I can find no rest
death to the fascist insect

the biggest action since Foster
Naga the seven-headed cobra
death to the fascist insect
that preys on the life of the people

Naga the seven-headed cobra
the interdependence of different species
that preys on the life of the people
there aren't any shortcuts to

the interdependence of different species
General Field Marshall Cinque Mtume
there aren't any shortcuts to
meaningful social change

General Field Marshall Cinque Mtume
America's most wanted
meaningful social change
I'm changing my name to Tania

America's most wanted
SLA feeds the poor
I'm changing my name to Tania
I have decided to stay and fight

SLA feeds the poor
People in Need
I have decided to stay and fight
a standard M1 carbine with a flashlight

People in Need
as long as the enemy exist
a standard M1 carbine with a flashlight
the most well-known female bank robber

Sallie-Anne

Just a junkie hooker
who couldn't pull the tail
from the snake's mouth

but she knows the cop
murdered her lover
and covered it up.
(Nothing is worse than
a crooked cop.)

He arranges a meeting
in Centennial Park,
a cast-iron bench
by a pool in the dark.

Next morning, dew
dapples the seat, gathers
and trickles down

past candy wrappers,
past a high-heeled sandal
lying on its side. It drips
into the pool

where ripples glide
and settle over
her wide open eyes,
her whistle-silenced lips.

Sonia

I never met Eric. George
loved me once. A decade later,
on his deathbed,
we married.

He expected me to save his life,
as once I'd brought life to his writing.
He modeled Julia on me.
A compliment, I thought, at first.
No longer.

The Euston Road Venus, the girl from
the fiction department; all different Sonia's
invented to fit their own needs.
No one noticed mine.

I took my responsibilities seriously;
editing 'Horizon', being a wife, acting as
George's literary trustee. My second husband
hid his sexuality from me. Until he went to jail,
and I faced it. A fool. Fooled.

That's when my life started going wrong,
though everything before that can be seen as
prelude to this slide into penury
and despond. Not a lot to be proud of.

Yes, I co-edited George's non-fiction works,
all four volumes of them, but I didn't write
original work myself. Now, homeless,
penniless, waiting on death in a hotel
whose bill won't be met, I wonder if
it was worth the bother. I'm glad it's over,
this silly dance of masks and shadows.

Tamara

This city is a book, a cage, a woman,
Queen of a Kingdom, its walls covered
in signs: messages, directions for Marco Polo,
erasures, holes, posters layering the history
of quelled rebellions. Exiled husband attacks,
backed by: Turkish forces, markets, harvests,
banks. Victory belongs to eyes of fresh water
pearls from an Oriental river.

Above the spate on a bleak crag a tower broods,
ancient, rocky. Light glows at night like sympathy
from a room at the top with a billowy bed, where
a woman, beauteous, legs spread, waits to ensnare
traveler or cavalier. She's also a virgin.

Farewell she calls. The traveler plunges to the river
or is pushed. Her voice is the voice of a woman,
a city, a cage, a Queen, the voice of an unopened
book on a shelf in the library that is this world;
faint weeping, tender
and sweet.

Virginia

Her world of air and water turned to stone;
on life's great stage she knew she'd missed a cue.
With timid steps she exited, alone.

Her words, like flesh, struck sweetest near the bone
where blood runs hot, and pain rebirths as new
her world. When air and water turned to stone,

tormented by the wrongs she can't atone,
she faced the truth she'd only tip-toed through
with timid steps. She exited alone

weighed down by failure. Harvests she had sown
became the famine that would soon undo
her world of air and water. Turned to stone,

she froze as time expired, white ashes blown
away like veils, exposing death's allure.
With timid steps she exited. Alone

she walked her garden one last time. Well-known
the path, the gate. One final sad adieu;
her words of air and water turned to stone,
with timid steps she exited alone.

Vita in their own words

I am reduced to a thing that wants Virginia.
I have come to the conclusion, after many years
of sometimes sad experience, that you cannot
come to any conclusion at all.

I really feel myself in my tower, shut away.
But that is not the whole story ... I wanted
to lead his life, parallel with the life of love,
separate, independent. He wanted to retain
his individuality, his activity, his timetable.

Julian, Mitya, David, Dark Man,
male, arrogant, alone, the bull.
My private sign, meaning Very Easy.
Few things are more distasteful than
veiled hints.

A damned outmoded poet.
They destroyed me forever.
My own image, within reach, beyond reach.
God knows, I gave you all my love.

I do get so frightfully, frenziedly excited
writing poetry. It is the only thing that
makes me truly and completely happy.
I really feel myself. My duality.

Homesick we are, and always, for
another and different world.
We owned a garden on a hill,
we planted rose and daffodil.

I *hate* safety, and would rather
fail gloriously than dingily succeed.
And still the strange meaningless
conversations continue.

I worshipped dead men for their strength,
forgetting I was strong.
I don't know what to say to you.
One must be businesslike, although
the glass is falling. Though you may wobble
in your orbit, you can never escape from it.

There was never anything but love
to keep us together, to clap the net
over the butterfly of the moment.
It is painful but also rather pleasant,

if you know what I mean.

The Wawalag Sisters

Way back in dreamtime, two sisters
coming home for a bunya nut ceremony
stopped to rest by a waterhole.

There, a baby was born.
The smell of blood woke
the snake that lived there.
This was his totem place.

He rose, and the plains flooded .
The sisters waited out the flood
on a rise. The snake reared up
and swallowed the camp: sisters,
baby, and fire.

He swam back to the bottom of the
billabong, but fire still burned inside him.
Bellowing with pain he fled, making a trail
that soon filled up, and became a river.

He spewed his stomach empty.
When the waters dried, the sisters
woke up, and set out again
with their baby, for their homeland.

Zelda

Edge of the void, seventh page
of a single volume. Pain.
They've stopped providing relief,
retuned reality to something I can't ignore;
technology that never was for me,
the white science projects of thought.

Some evenings ago – did I forget?
Did I? Forget? I saw. Fireflies
took off from this fence right here,
flew steadily into what was not light.

I stopped remembering many times,
became hopeless at it. The sun moved
to vertical, I hated how it controlled
my shadow by coming closer. It
reminded me the void's not always viable.

The sun began its moon phase
and the next dancer straightened herself
like a ladder. (Tail lights stream together
like fireflies. Silence increases
as visitors vanish.)

I thought they took me in
to help a friend, not to torment.
I've found most enemies live
in sea breezes, in bell's bellies,
in freight liner sirens –

Was I brave?
Was I brave? Yes, sort of. No,
but I stopped at the edges of beaches
and listened anyway, challenged the science
of secrets, folded and hidden.

During dawn in the writing process, we
worked together. Then something picked
me up, set me down without touching,
like a magnet, two poles from where I'd
failed. Staying passive damaged
the science of speech.

Didn't I know that peacocks roost?
Didn't I know that anything will dance
if the drum machine is set to 'start'?
I intuit a stranger's reflection in my mirror.
I wonder who I am now. Time's technology.

I ended up like this. They took my mind.
When I arrived they tortured me
so meticulously it felt like racking up credit;
from my dancing and singing they took
the music. From my memory ...

No one escapes. I stayed. I lived.
Some fell like snow; they melted
in crochets and quavers, mists floating
around the stage as I faced the crowd.

I could have kept dancing. I didn't
know that. I didn't have to give it up.
Dance could have saved me. They keep me
folded inside all the darkened reflections
I thought could never damage my world.

I pretended repentance. Like a star dissected
and saved in a test tube, I became ashamed
of absence, ashamed of presence, yet I always
expected the sacrifice required. I went to them
willingly, both father and husband. I just
couldn't stay there.

Notes and Acknowledgements

After Goldilocks

A variation of a 19th-century fairy tale. The story was first recorded in
narrative form by British writer and poet Robert Southey, and first published
anonymously as "The Story of the Three Bears" in 1837 in a volume of his
writings called *The Doctor*. It has been interpreted and adapted ever since.

My version published in Danse Macabre Online Issue #112

Amelia

Amelia Earhardt was an American pioneer aviator and author. She
disappeared in July 1937 over the Pacific Ocean near New Guinea. No
authenticated trace of her plane has been found, though searches still
continue.

Published in 4th Floor 2017

Anais

Anais Nin, an American author born in France of Cuban parents, known
mostly for her extensive journals, her erotica, and her 'simultaneous
marriages' to Guiler and Pole.

Published in Otoliths July 2016

Anne Sexton, listening to the devil

Anne Sexton, American poet, a pioneer of 'confessional' poetry, Pulitzer Prize
winner in 1967 for her book *Live or Die*. My poem is after 'For Eleanor
Boylan, talking to God' by Anne Sexton.

Published in Danse Macabre Online Issue #112

Annie

Annie Oakley, American sharpshooter and exhibition shooter who toured
America, and the world, with Buffalo Bill's Wild West Show. She performed
before royalty and heads of state. My poem is a found poem, from the text of
the wikipedia page Annie Oakley.

Published in Danse Macabre Online Issue #112

Antigone

In Greek mythology the daughter/sister of Oedipus and his wife. Versions of
her story form part of works by Sophocles, Euripides, and Hyginis, and she is
depicted in ancient paintings and on vases.

Published in Danse Macabre Online Issue #112

Some Bessie blues (for Jan) -

Bessie Smith, black American blues singer known as The Empress of the Blues in 1920/30's. The most famous female blues singer of her time, she influenced other musicians including Janis Joplin, who bought and installed a headstone on Bessie's grave. (Jan is my sister-in-law, another blues and jazz singer/musician.)

It is a list poem, referencing the titles of all the songs Bessie recorded during her career.

Published in Danse Macabre Online Issue #112

Jane Bowles

American writer and playwright, wife of the writer Paul Bowles (*The Sheltering Sky*). His novel depicts their life together in Tangiers. She was also bisexual, an alcoholic, and suffered a stroke at age 40, which affected her ability to write. Tennessee Williams, Truman Capote, and John Ashbery, all highly praised her work.

Published in Otoliths February 2018

Cleopatra's suicide soliloquy

Cleopatra VII was the last pharoah of Egypt. Her liasons with Julius Caesar, and later Mark Antony, protected Egypt's independence. Mark Anthony was defeated in battle by Octavian, and committed suicide. Cleopatra joined him and Egypt became a province of Rome. (Egyptian poet Cavafy wrote about the God abandoning Antony, and Leonard Cohen made Cavafy's poem into his song 'Alexandra leaving'.)

Published in Otoliths February 2018

CoCo

Gabrielle Bonheur "Coco" Chanel was a French fashion designer who revolutionized the way women dressed after WWI, freeing them from constraints of girdle and hobble skirt. Her designs were elegant, comfortable, practical, easy to wear. Using new fabrics like jersey, she set the standard for modern fashion for the next eighty years. Other Chanel lines include shoes, faux jewelry, handbags, and of course, perfume. She spent WWII holed up in the Ritz in Paris with her lover, a German spy, but was never charged as a collaborator.

Published in Broadsheet 21

Effie

Euphemia Chalmers "Effie" Millais, Lady Millais née Gray, was the wife of critic John Ruskin, though their marriage was never consummated. She left him and later married his protege, the Pre-Raphaelite painter John Everett Millais. This Victorian love triangle was the focus of much gossip and speculation, and has been immortalized in plays, films, and an opera.

Published in Otoliths February 2018

Frida grieves

Magdalena Carmen Frida Kahlo y Calderón, more commonly known as Frida Kahlo, Mexican artist, wife of Diego Rivera. A communist, she welcomed Leon Trotsky to sanctuary in Mexico, and became his lover. She was injured in a street-car accident as a teenager and suffered all her life from its effects. Known for her self-portaits, with her iconic 'monobrow', often painted while she was lying flat in bed. She dressed in indigenous costumes from her home province, Coyoacan, explored questions of gender, class and race in Mexican society in her work, and was the first Mexican artist featured in the Louvre's collection.

Georgia O'Keeffe 1918

Georgia Totto O'Keeffe, American artist, known as 'the mother of American modernism'. She painted many oversized flowers, and landscapes of New York, and New Mexico. Art dealer and photographer Alfred Stieglitz held an exhibition of her work. She moved to New York at his request, gave up teaching and concentrated on painting. They married in 1924. She spent part of each year after 1929 in the South West. She was the first woman artist to have a retrospective at the Museum of Modern Art (MoMA) in Manhattan. In 2014 a painting of hers, Jimson weed, sold for $44,000,000.

Yes, very alien, Gertrude

Gertrude Stein was an American playwright, poet, novelist, and art collector. She moved to Paris in 1903 with her long-time companion, Alice B. Toklas. Her salon was frequented by leading figures of modernism in literature and art, including Pablo Picasso, Ernest Hemingway, F. Scott Fitzgerald, Sinclair Lewis, Ezra Pound, and Henri Matisse. She wrote mostly in a highly idiosyncratic, repetitive style that echoed the visual art of the times. One of the first writers to look at queer and feminist politics, her other political views, re immigration, sound racist today.

The form is an erasure poem from page 214 of Gertrude Stein's *Look at me now and here I am,* writings and lectures 1911 - 1945 edited by Patricia Meyerowitz (excerpt from A Valentine to Sherwood Anderson)

Published in Otoliths July 2016

The girl who won't smile

Approximately 24,300 girls and 22,900 women whose homes were destroyed
or severely damaged during the hostilities in 2014, remain displaced in
precarious conditions. Most of the children in Gaza have lost family
members to Israeli attacks.
Many of the children are severely traumatised.

The form is an Italian or Petrarchan sonnet.

Grendel

As a child, I was curious about my grandmother's wood stove, and she told
me a dragon called Grendel lived in the firebox, and would eat me if I came
too near. When I read translations of Beowulf, decades later, Grendel felt like
an old friend.

Published inWalt's Corner, a poetry column in The Long Islander (founded
        by Walt Whitman 1839)

Henrietta Lacks

Born Loretta Pleasant, she was an African-American woman who died of
cervical cancer in 1951. Cells from her tumor were biopsied, and cultured by
George Gey, to become the HeLa cell line, the first immortalised cell line, still
used in medical research. She was not asked for consent to take the cells, and
her family were not compensated for their use.

The form is a Ballade.

Published in Otoliths February 2016

Hillary's collections

Hillary Baxter, poet, and daughter of poets and writers James K. Baxter and
Jacqui Sturm, lived in Paekakariki at the end of her life. Unable to work for
medical reasons, she kept groups of collected or created objects, all quite
small, displayed on her living-room floor, and spent a lot of time arranging,
rearranging, and changing these displays. They reminded me of the way a
writer plays with words.

Hinemoa

The legend of Hinemoa, and Tutanakei, her lover, was first collected by Sir
George Grey in his *Polynesian Mythology*. It tells of Hinemoa's swim across
Lake Rotorua to Molokai Island, to meet with her lover, after her tribe had
hidden all the canoes so she couldn't paddle there. Despite the ambiguity of
my poem, she made it, and the lovers did, in legend, live 'happily ever after'.

Katherine Mansfield

New Zealand born, she lived England or Europe for most of her life, writing of the home she had left, and the people there. She travelled often in search of a cure for a disease that eventually killed her at a young age. Her writing was much admired by Virginia Woolf. After her death her husband, John Middleton Murry, edited and published more work. Her short life has been portrayed in films, biographies, and novels, and the Menton Fellowship has been established for NZ writers to spend a year writing in her room at Menton.

The form is a list poem, documenting places she lived, in chronological order.

Published in Otoliths July 2016

Russian New Year with Gurdjieff

Katherine Mansfield sought respite as a guest at Gurdjieff's establishment outside Paris, in the last few months of her life, and died there, 9 January 1923.

Published in 4th Floor 2014

Leni

Leni Riefenstahl was a German film director, producer, screenwriter, editor, photographer, actress, and dancer, who pioneered methods of filming still used today. Hitler commissioned her to work on various propoganda projects for the Third Reich, including documenting his rallies. She was unpopular after the war because of her close association with Hitler, and for insisting that the gypsies she used in one film made during the war were all still alive at war's end. Throughout her life she denied knowledge of the Holocaust. She wrote an autobiography and several books about the Nuba people in Africa before dying aged 101.

* final stanza is a quote from Leni Riefenstahl in a 1980s BBC interview.

Lilith

In Jewish folk-lore Lilith was the first wife of Adam, made at the same time and from the same materials. She seems to be a remnant of ancient Mesopotamian religion and was depicted as a demon in: the Old Testament book of Isaiah, the Dead Sea Scrolls, and magical talismans from around 600CE. She appeared in Goethe's *Faust,* which influenced Dante Gabriel Rosetti's painting of her, with a sonnet dedicated to her. Sometimes confused with Lamia.

The form is an Italian or Petrarchan sonnet.

Malala

Malala Yousafzai is a Pakistani activist for education of women, women's rights, and children's rights. Nobel Peace Prize in 2014, at the age of 17, the youngest ever Nobel Prize laureate. At 12 she wrote a blog for BBC Urdu about life during the Taliban occupation of Swat, and a New York Times documentary spread her story further. In October 2012 a Taliban tribesman attempted to murder her, which sparked an international outpouring of support for her work. She recovered, probably the most well-known teenager in the world, and continued her work, founding the not-for-profit Malala Fund to fianance her activism. She has addressed the United Nations, written a memoir *I am Malala,* and has been the recipient of many awards and honorary degrees worldwide, and the subject of an award-winning documentary.

The form is an English or Shakesperean sonnet, and the final line is the final line from W. B. Yeats' poem *Among School Children.*

The Margaret Collection

Margaret and Warren were my neighbours in a Sydney inner-city suburb, in a line of bald-faced terraced houses hidden behind Chinatown in Ultimo. The corner house had been the birthplace of Darcy Dugan, Australian petty criminal, who worked to work on his first job, robbing the bank on Harris Street. The last stanza in the first section is a quote from an old NSW Health Department publication. The terraces dated from 1820, built for the staff of the Governor's stables.

Published in Issue #33 of Clockwise Cat 2016

Marie

Maria Salomea Skłodowska, Marie Curie, a Polish-born, French-nationalized physicist and chemist who became the first woman to win the Nobel Prize, and the first and only woman to win it twice, in two different sciences. She died due to aplastic anemia brought on by exposure to radiation while carrying test tubes of radium in her pockets.

The execution of Mary, Queen of Scots

Mary Stuart, Mary I of Scotland, daughter of James V, acceded to the throne at 6 days old. She was later forced to abdicate in favour of her year-old son James VI and sought the protection of her second cousin once removed, Queen Elizabeth I of England who imprisoned her, fearing for her own throne. After almost nineteen years in custody she was beheaded.

Mary Tudor's madrigal

Also known as Bloody Mary, she was the only surviving child of Henry VIII and Catherine of Aragon. Taking the throne after the death of her half-brother Edward VI and the beheading of Lady Jane Grey who had been proclaimed Queen, she restored Roman Catholicism as England's religion. She ruled for five years, and her successor, younger half-sister Elizabeth I, daughter of Henry VIII and Anne Boleyn, restored Protestantism to England.

The form is an English madrigal.

Meenybradden lady

Meenybradden Woman was a bog body, found in County Donegal, Ireland, in 1978, and dated to between 1050 to 1410CE. I decided she was a lady.

The form is a sestina.

Published in 4th Floor 2017

Mileva

Mileva Marić, sometimes called Mileva Marić-Einstein or Mileva Marić-Ajnštajn, was a Serbian physicist. She was a fellow student (the only woman in the class) of Albert Einstein. They had a daughter who died in 1903, and married after that. They later had two sons. Her contribution to Einstein's theories is disputed and much discussed still.

Published in Jaam #33 2015

Patti snaps from the M train

A found poem from the text of *M Train,* a book by Patti Smith. She is an American musician, artist, poet, author, who recently faltered while playing Bob Dylan's song *A hard rains's goin' to fall,* at the ceremony that awarded him a Nobel Prize in literature.

Patty Hearst

Patricia Campbell "Patty" Hearst (now known as Patty Hearst Shaw), granddaughter of American publishing magnate William Randolph Hearst, was kidnapped by the Simbionese Liberation Army as a nineteen-year-old student and, after isolation and death threats, supported their cause and joined them in propaganda and bank robberies. Arrested after nineteen months, she was convicted of bank robbery but her sentence was commuted by President Jimmy Carter and she was pardoned by President Bill Clinton.

The form is a pantoum, found in press interviews with and articles about her. The repeats suit her connection with newspapers, through her grandfather, I thought.

Sallie -Anne

Sallie-Anne Huckstepp, Australian prostitue, heroin addict, writer and whistleblower. She claimed rogue NSW detective Roger Rogerson had murdered her lover Warren Lanfranchi, and stolen the cash he was carrying to bribe Rogerson. She told friends she feared Rogerson would kill her. At the inquest, her death was found to have been caused by a person or persons unknown.

Sonia

Sonia Mary Brownell, better known as Sonia Orwell, was the second wife of Eric Blair, who wrote as George Orwell. The character Julia in 1984 was modeled on her. She became Orwell's literary executor after his death and died of a brain tumor, penniless.

Tamara

Tamara is a city in Italo Calvino's novel *Invisible Cities* which explores imagination through the description of cities visited by Marco Polo. The city was named for Queen Tamar of Georgia, whose reputation was shredded by men who tried to control her and her country.

Virginia

Virginia Woolf, British author, part of the Bloomsbury Group. She suffered from depression all her adult life, and committed suicide by walking into a river with her pockets weighed with stones.

Published in 4th Floor 2017

Vita in their own words

Victoria Mary Sackville-West, Lady Nicolson, known as Vita Sackville-West, was a British poet, novelist, journalist, and garden designer. Bisexual, she assumed different male characters, and had a decade-long affair with Virginia Woolf. She was the inspiration for the androgynous Orlando in Virginia's novel *Orlando: A biography.*

Form is a found poem from letters from Vita to Virginia, and interviews with Vita.

The Wawalag Sisters

An aboriginal myth of the Yolngu from the Arnhem Land area of Australia. Different versions of it exist, both as a Creation Myth explaining the course of a river, and as a ceremonial symbol of the attainment of manhood by boys (the regurgitation).

Zelda

Zelda Fitzgerald was an American novelist, socialite, and wife of the author F Scott Fitzgerald. She and Scott became emblems of the Jazz Age. They both drank heavily, fought, and had numerous affairs outside the marriage. Her diaries provided much of the material in Scott's novels. Diagnosed with manic depression, she spent time in and out of specialist clinics for decades. They were living apart when Scott died suddenly, in 1940. She died in a fire at her hospital seven years later.

Author notes

Since graduating MA from IIML Victoria University Wellington in 2011 Mercedes has been extensively published world-wide, with more than 400 poems to her credit. She lives on the Kapiti Coast, New Zealand.

www.ingramcontent.com/pod-product-compliance
Lightning Source LLC
Chambersburg PA
CBHW051009060726
47593CB00017B/1273